# TROMBONE

# 101 DISNEY SONGS

Available for
FLUTE, CLARINET, ALTO SAX, TENOR SAX, TRUMPET,
HORN, TROMBONE, VIOLIN, VIOLA, CELLO

ISBN 978-1-5400-0239-6

The following songs are the property of:

Bourne Co.
Music Publishers
5 West 37th Street
New York, NY 10018

BABY MINE
GIVE A LITTLE WHISTLE
HEIGH-HO
HI-DIDDLE-DEE-DEE (AN ACTOR'S LIFE FOR ME)
I'M WISHING
I'VE GOT NO STRINGS
SOME DAY MY PRINCE WILL COME
WHEN I SEE AN ELEPHANT FLY
WHEN YOU WISH UPON A STAR
WHISTLE WHILE YOU WORK
WHO'S AFRAID OF THE BIG BAD WOLF?
WITH A SMILE AND A SONG

DISTRIBUTED BY

7777 W. BLUEMOUND RD. P.O. BOX 13819 MILWAUKEE, WI 53213

Visit Hal Leonard Online at
**www.halleonard.com**

# CONTENTS

4 Baby Mine

4 The Ballad of Davy Crockett

6 Be Our Guest

7 Beauty and the Beast

5 Bella Notte

8 Belle

12 Best of Friends

9 Bibbidi-Bobbidi-Boo (The Magic Song)

10 Breaking Free

13 Can You Feel the Love Tonight

14 Candle on the Water

15 Chim Chim Cher-ee

16 Circle of Life

17 The Climb

20 Colors of the Wind

18 Cruella De Vil

22 Days in the Sun

21 Do You Want to Build a Snowman?

18 A Dream Is a Wish Your Heart Makes

24 Evermore

19 Feed the Birds (Tuppence a Bag)

26 For the First Time in Forever

28 Friend Like Me

30 Gaston

33 Give a Little Whistle

34 Go the Distance

32 God Help the Outcasts

35 Hakuna Matata

36 Happy Working Song

38 He's a Pirate

39 He's a Tramp

25 Heigh-Ho

27 Hi-Diddle-Dee-Dee (An Actor's Life for Me)

40 How Does a Moment Last Forever

42 How Far I'll Go

41 I Just Can't Wait to Be King

44 I See the Light

46 I'll Make a Man Out of You

43 I'm Late

45 I'm Wishing

48 I've Got a Dream

54 I've Got No Strings

50 If I Can't Love Her

52 If I Never Knew You (End Title)

47 In Summer

54 It's a Small World

55 Kiss the Girl

56 Lava

60 Lavender Blue (Dilly Dilly)

58 Let It Go

61 Let's Go Fly a Kite

62 The Lord Is Good to Me

57 Love Is an Open Door

60 Mickey Mouse March

66 Mother Knows Best

62 My Funny Friend and Me

64 Part of Your World

66 A Pirate's Life

68 Reflection

67 Rumbly in My Tumbly*

69 The Second Star to the Right

70 Seize the Day

74 The Siamese Cat Song

72 So Close

71 So This Is Love

74 Some Day My Prince Will Come

75 Someday

76 Something There

77 A Spoonful of Sugar

78 Supercalifragilisticexpialidocious

80 That's How You Know

79 "This is me."

81 Toyland March

82 Trashin' the Camp (Pop Version)**

84 True Love's Kiss

83 The Unbirthday Song

86 We Belong Together

88 We Know the Way

90 We're All in This Together

85 Westward Ho, the Wagons!

89 A Whale of a Tale

87 When I See an Elephant Fly

92 When She Loved Me

94 When Will My Life Begin?

93 When You Wish Upon a Star

91 Whistle While You Work

96 Who's Afraid of the Big Bad Wolf?

98 A Whole New World

97 Winnie the Pooh*

95 With a Smile and a Song

100 The Wonderful Thing About Tiggers*

102 Written in the Stars

100 Yo Ho (A Pirate's Life for Me)

104 You Are the Music in Me

103 You Can Fly! You Can Fly! You Can Fly!

106 You'll Be in My Heart (Pop Version)**

108 You're Welcome

112 You've Got a Friend in Me

110 Zero to Hero

109 Zip-A-Dee-Doo-Dah

101 Theme from Zorro

*Based on the "Winnie the Pooh" works,
by A. A. Milne and E. H. Shepard

**TARZAN® Owned by Edgar Rice Burroughs, Inc.
and Used by Permission.
© Burroughs/Disney

# BABY MINE
## from DUMBO

TROMBONE

Words by NED WASHINGTON
Music by FRANK CHURCHILL

# THE BALLAD OF DAVY CROCKETT
## from DAVY CROCKETT

Words by TOM BLACKBURN
Music by GEORGE BRUNS

# BELLA NOTTE
from LADY AND THE TRAMP

Music and Lyrics by PEGGY LEE
and SONNY BURKE

**Slowly**

TROMBONE

# BE OUR GUEST
from BEAUTY AND THE BEAST

Music by ALAN MENKEN
Lyrics by HOWARD ASHMAN

# BEAUTY AND THE BEAST

from BEAUTY AND THE BEAST

TROMBONE

Music by ALAN MENKEN
Lyrics by HOWARD ASHMAN

**Moderately slow**

# BELLE
### from BEAUTY AND THE BEAST

TROMBONE

Music by ALAN MENKEN
Lyrics by HOWARD ASHMAN

# BIBBIDI-BOBBIDI-BOO
(The Magic Song)
from CINDERELLA

Words by JERRY LIVINGSTON
Music by MACK DAVID and AL HOFFMAN

**Brightly**

# BREAKING FREE
from HIGH SCHOOL MUSICAL

TROMBONE

Words and Music by
JAMIE HOUSTON

**Moderately**

# BEST OF FRIENDS
from THE FOX AND THE HOUND

TROMBONE

Words by STAN FIDEL
Music by RICHARD JOHNSTON

**Moderately**

# CAN YOU FEEL THE LOVE TONIGHT

from THE LION KING

TROMBONE

Music by ELTON JOHN
Lyrics by TIM RICE

**Pop Ballad**

# CANDLE ON THE WATER

from PETE'S DRAGON

TROMBONE

Words and Music by AL KASHA
and JOEL HIRSCHHORN

# CHIM CHIM CHER-EE

from MARY POPPINS

**TROMBONE**

Words and Music by RICHARD M. SHERMAN
and ROBERT B. SHERMAN

**Lightly, with gusto**

small notes optional

# CIRCLE OF LIFE
from THE LION KING

TROMBONE

Music by ELTON JOHN
Lyrics by TIM RICE

**Moderately (with an African beat)**

# THE CLIMB

from HANNAH MONTANA: THE MOVIE

**TROMBONE**

Words and Music by JESSI ALEXANDER
and JON MABE

**Moderately slow**

# CRUELLA DE VIL
from 101 DALMATIANS

TROMBONE

Words and Music by
MEL LEVEN

**Slow Blues**

# A DREAM IS A WISH YOUR HEART MAKES
from CINDERELLA

Words and Music by MACK DAVID,
AL HOFFMAN and JERRY LIVINGSTON

**Moderately**

# FEED THE BIRDS
(Tuppence a Bag)

from MARY POPPINS

Words and Music by RICHARD M. SHERMAN
and ROBERT B. SHERMAN

# COLORS OF THE WIND
from POCAHONTAS

TROMBONE

Music by ALAN MENKEN
Lyrics by STEPHEN SCHWARTZ

# DO YOU WANT TO BUILD A SNOWMAN?

from FROZEN

TROMBONE

Music and Lyrics by KRISTEN ANDERSON-LOPEZ
and ROBERT LOPEZ

# DAYS IN THE SUN
from BEAUTY AND THE BEAST

**TROMBONE**

Music by ALAN MENKEN
Lyrics by TIM RICE

**Moderately**

# EVERMORE
from BEAUTY AND THE BEAST

**TROMBONE**

Music by ALAN MENKEN
Lyrics by TIM RICE

**Moderately**

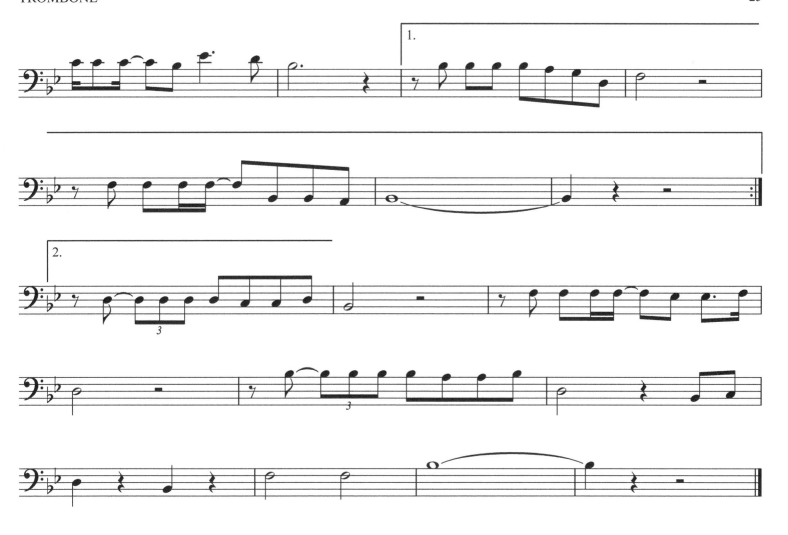

# HEIGH-HO
## (The Dwarfs' Marching Song)
### from SNOW WHITE AND THE SEVEN DWARFS

Words by LARRY MOREY
Music by FRANK CHURCHILL

**Brightly, cheerfully**

# FOR THE FIRST TIME IN FOREVER

from FROZEN

TROMBONE

Music and Lyrics by KRISTEN ANDERSON-LOPEZ
and ROBERT LOPEZ

**Moderately, with excitement**

**Moderately, with expression**

# HI-DIDDLE-DEE-DEE

(An Actor's Life for Me)

from PINOCCHIO

Words by NED WASHINGTON
Music by LEIGH HARLINE

**Brightly, in 2**

# FRIEND LIKE ME

from ALADDIN

TROMBONE

Music by ALAN MENKEN
Lyrics by HOWARD ASHMAN

# GASTON
from BEAUTY AND THE BEAST

**TROMBONE**

Music by ALAN MENKEN
Lyrics by HOWARD ASHMAN

# GOD HELP THE OUTCASTS

from THE HUNCHBACK OF NOTRE DAME

**TROMBONE**

Music by ALAN MENKEN
Lyrics by STEPHEN SCHWARTZ

# GIVE A LITTLE WHISTLE
from PINOCCHIO

Words by NED WASHINGTON
Music by LEIGH HARLINE

**Moderately, in 2**

# GO THE DISTANCE
from HERCULES

TROMBONE

Music by ALAN MENKEN
Lyrics by DAVID ZIPPEL

**Slowly**

# HAKUNA MATATA

from THE LION KING

TROMBONE

Music by ELTON JOHN
Lyrics by TIM RICE

# HAPPY WORKING SONG
from ENCHANTED

TROMBONE

Music by ALAN MENKEN
Lyrics by STEPHEN SCHWARTZ

# HE'S A PIRATE
from PIRATES OF THE CARIBBEAN: THE CURSE OF THE BLACK PEARL

TROMBONE

Music by KLAUS BADELT,
GEOFFREY ZANELLI and HANS ZIMMER

# HE'S A TRAMP
from LADY AND THE TRAMP

Words and Music by PEGGY LEE
and SONNY BURKE

**Moderately**

# HOW DOES A MOMENT LAST FOREVER

from BEAUTY AND THE BEAST

TROMBONE

Music by ALAN MENKEN
Lyrics by TIM RICE

**Moderately**

# I JUST CAN'T WAIT TO BE KING

from THE LION KING

TROMBONE

Music by ELTON JOHN
Lyrics by TIM RICE

# HOW FAR I'LL GO

from MOANA

**TROMBONE**

Music and Lyrics by
LIN-MANUEL MIRANDA

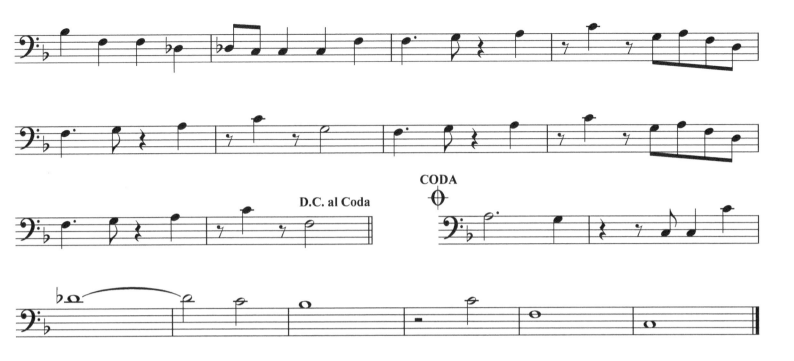

# I'M LATE

from ALICE IN WONDERLAND

Words by BOB HILLIARD
Music by SAMMY FAIN

# I SEE THE LIGHT

from TANGLED

TROMBONE

Music by ALAN MENKEN
Lyrics by GLENN SLATER

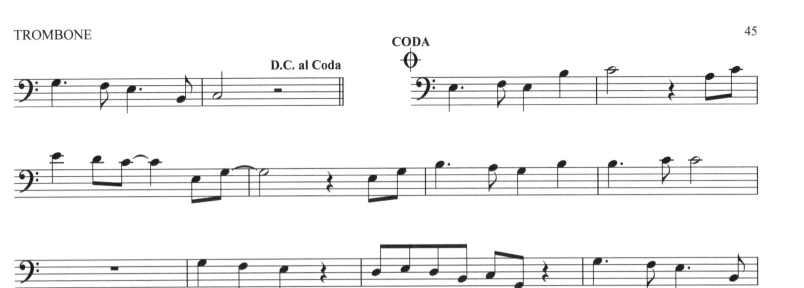

# I'M WISHING
from SNOW WHITE AND THE SEVEN DWARFS

Words by LARRY MOREY
Music by FRANK CHURCHILL

**Moderately slow, in 2**

# I'LL MAKE A MAN OUT OF YOU

from MULAN

TROMBONE

Music by MATTHEW WILDER
Lyrics by DAVID ZIPPEL

**Moderately**

# IN SUMMER
from FROZEN

TROMBONE

Music and Lyrics by KRISTEN ANDERSON-LOPEZ
and ROBERT LOPEZ

**Moderately, in 2**

# I'VE GOT A DREAM
from TANGLED

TROMBONE

Music by ALAN MENKEN
Lyrics by GLENN SLATER

**Moderately fast**

# IF I CAN'T LOVE HER

from BEAUTY AND THE BEAST: THE BROADWAY MUSICAL

**TROMBONE**

Music by ALAN MENKEN
Lyrics by TIM RICE

# IF I NEVER KNEW YOU
### (End Title)
from POCAHONTAS

TROMBONE

Music by ALAN MENKEN
Lyrics by STEPHEN SCHWARTZ

**Moderately slow**

# I'VE GOT NO STRINGS
from PINOCCHIO

TROMBONE

Words by NED WASHINGTON
Music by LEIGH HARLINE

# IT'S A SMALL WORLD
from Disney Parks' "it's a small world" attraction

Words and Music by RICHARD M. SHERMAN
and ROBERT B. SHERMAN

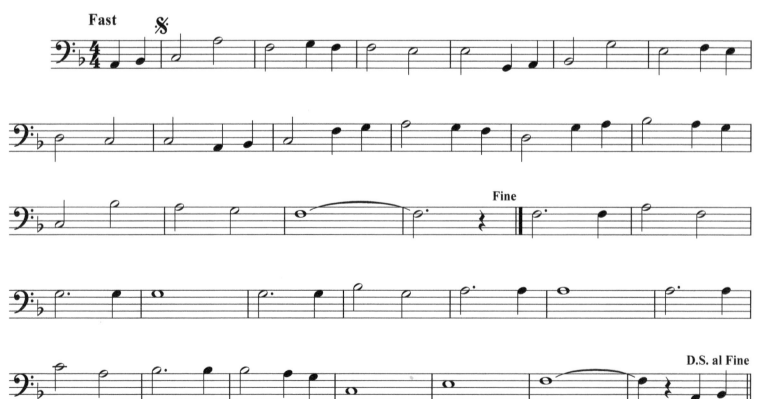

# KISS THE GIRL
from THE LITTLE MERMAID

**TROMBONE**

Music by ALAN MENKEN
Lyrics by HOWARD ASHMAN

**Moderately**

To Coda

**CODA**

**D.C. al Coda**

# LAVA
from LAVA

**TROMBONE**

Music and Lyrics by
JAMES FORD MURPHY

**Moderately slow, in 2**

# LOVE IS AN OPEN DOOR

from FROZEN

TROMBONE

Music and Lyrics by KRISTEN ANDERSON-LOPEZ
and ROBERT LOPEZ

# LET IT GO
### from FROZEN

TROMBONE

Music and Lyrics by KRISTEN ANDERSON-LOPEZ
and ROBERT LOPEZ

# LAVENDER BLUE
## (Dilly Dilly)
### from SO DEAR TO MY HEART

TROMBONE

Words by LARRY MOREY
Music by ELIOT DANIEL

# MICKEY MOUSE MARCH
### from THE MICKEY MOUSE CLUB

Words and Music by
JIMMIE DODD

# LET'S GO FLY A KITE

from MARY POPPINS

Words and Music by RICHARD M. SHERMAN
and ROBERT B. SHERMAN

**With gusto**

# THE LORD IS GOOD TO ME
from MELODY TIME

TROMBONE

Words and Music by KIM GANNON
and WALTER KENT

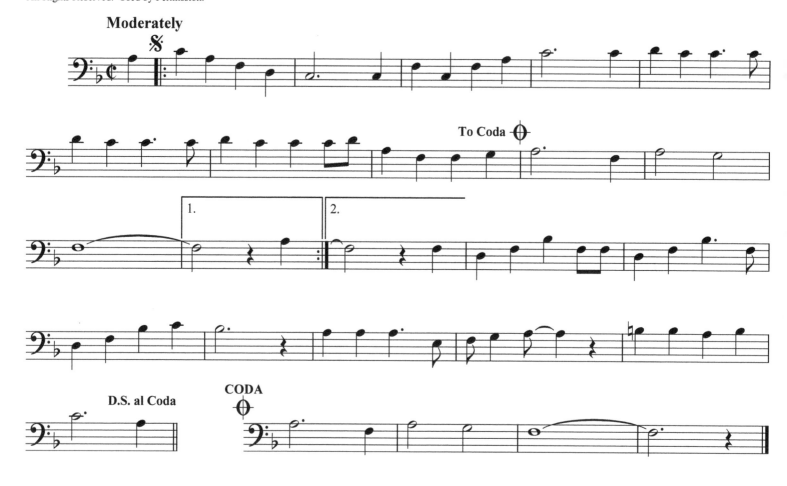

# MY FUNNY FRIEND AND ME
from THE EMPEROR'S NEW GROOVE

Lyrics by STING
Music by STING and DAVID HARTLEY

# PART OF YOUR WORLD
from THE LITTLE MERMAID

TROMBONE

Music by ALAN MENKEN
Lyrics by HOWARD ASHMAN

**Moderately bright**

# MOTHER KNOWS BEST
## from TANGLED

**TROMBONE**

Music by ALAN MENKEN
Lyrics by GLENN SLATER

**Moderately slow, in 2**

# A PIRATE'S LIFE
## from PETER PAN

Words by ED PENNER
Music by OLIVER WALLACE

**Moderately, with a bounce**

# RUMBLY IN MY TUMBLY

from THE MANY ADVENTURES OF WINNIE THE POOH

Words and Music by RICHARD M. SHERMAN
and ROBERT B. SHERMAN

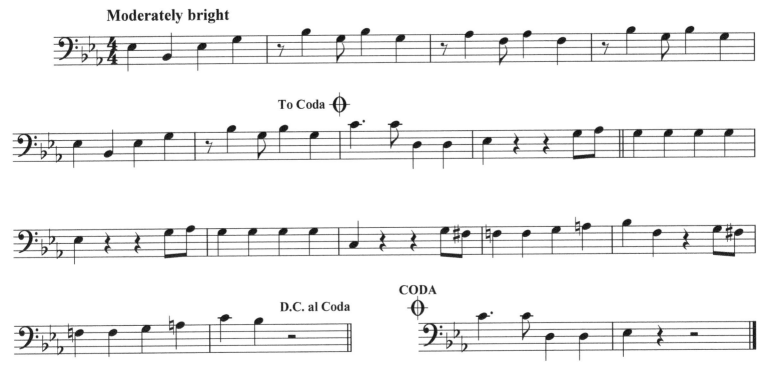

# REFLECTION
from MULAN

TROMBONE

Music by MATTHEW WILDER
Lyrics by DAVID ZIPPEL

# THE SECOND STAR TO THE RIGHT

from PETER PAN

Words by SAMMY CAHN
Music by SAMMY FAIN

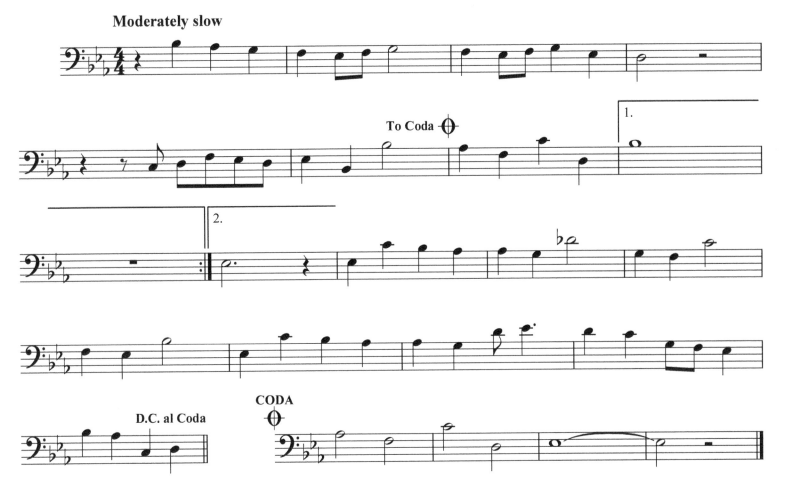

# SEIZE THE DAY
### from NEWSIES

TROMBONE

Music by ALAN MENKEN
Lyrics by JACK FELDMAN

# SO THIS IS LOVE
## from CINDERELLA

**TROMBONE**

Words and Music by AL HOFFMAN,
MACK DAVID and JERRY LIVINGSTON

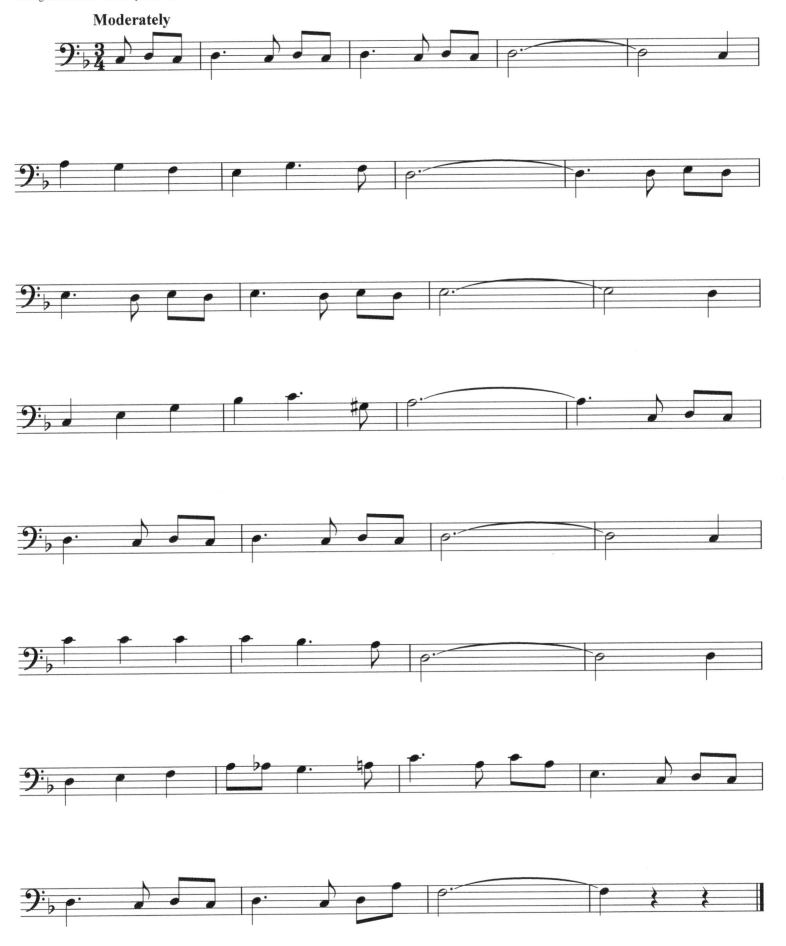

# SO CLOSE
from ENCHANTED

TROMBONE

Music by ALAN MENKEN
Lyrics by STEPHEN SCHWARTZ

**Moderately slow, in 4**

*small note optional*

1.

2.

# THE SIAMESE CAT SONG
from LADY AND THE TRAMP

TROMBONE

Words and Music by PEGGY LEE
and SONNY BURKE

**Slowly**

# SOME DAY MY PRINCE WILL COME
from SNOW WHITE AND THE SEVEN DWARFS

Words by LARRY MOREY
Music by FRANK CHURCHILL

**Moderately**

# SOMEDAY
### from THE HUNCHBACK OF NOTRE DAME

**TROMBONE**

Music by ALAN MENKEN
Lyrics by STEPHEN SCHWARTZ

# SOMETHING THERE

from BEAUTY AND THE BEAST

TROMBONE

Music by ALAN MENKEN
Lyrics by HOWARD ASHMAN

# A SPOONFUL OF SUGAR
from MARY POPPINS

TROMBONE

Words and Music by RICHARD M. SHERMAN
and ROBERT B. SHERMAN

# SUPERCALIFRAGILISTICEXPIALIDOCIOUS

from MARY POPPINS

TROMBONE

Words and Music by RICHARD M. SHERMAN
and ROBERT B. SHERMAN

# "THIS IS ME."
from RATATOUILLE

TROMBONE

Music by MICHAEL GIACCHINO

# THAT'S HOW YOU KNOW
from ENCHANTED

TROMBONE

Music by ALAN MENKEN
Lyrics by STEPHEN SCHWARTZ

# TOYLAND MARCH
from BABES IN TOYLAND

Adapted from V. HERBERT Melody
Words by MEL LEVEN
Music by GEORGE BRUNS

**March tempo**

# TRASHIN' THE CAMP
### (Pop Version)
from TARZAN™

TROMBONE

Words and Music by
PHIL COLLINS

# THE UNBIRTHDAY SONG
from ALICE IN WONDERLAND

TROMBONE

Words and Music by MACK DAVID,
AL HOFFMAN and JERRY LIVINGSTON

**Brightly**

# TRUE LOVE'S KISS
## from ENCHANTED

TROMBONE

Music by ALAN MENKEN
Lyrics by STEPHEN SCHWARTZ

**Moderately**

**Bright Waltz**

# WESTWARD HO, THE WAGONS!
from WESTWARD HO, THE WAGONS!

Words by TOM BLACKBURN
Music by GEORGE BRUNS

# WE BELONG TOGETHER
from TOY STORY 3

TROMBONE

Music and Lyrics by
RANDY NEWMAN

# WHEN I SEE AN ELEPHANT FLY

from DUMBO

Words by NED WASHINGTON
Music by OLIVER WALLACE

**Moderately fast**

# WE KNOW THE WAY

from MOANA

**TROMBONE**

Music by OPETAIA FOA'I
Lyrics by OPETAIA FOA'I
and LIN-MANUEL MIRANDA

**Moderately**

# A WHALE OF A TALE

from 20,000 LEAGUES UNDER THE SEA

**TROMBONE**

Words and Music by NORMAN GIMBEL
and AL HOFFMAN

**With a bounce**

# WE'RE ALL IN THIS TOGETHER

from HIGH SCHOOL MUSICAL

TROMBONE

Words and Music by MATTHEW GERRARD
and ROBBIE NEVIL

# WHISTLE WHILE YOU WORK

from SNOW WHITE AND THE SEVEN DWARFS

Words by LARRY MOREY
Music by FRANK CHURCHILL

**Moderately bright**

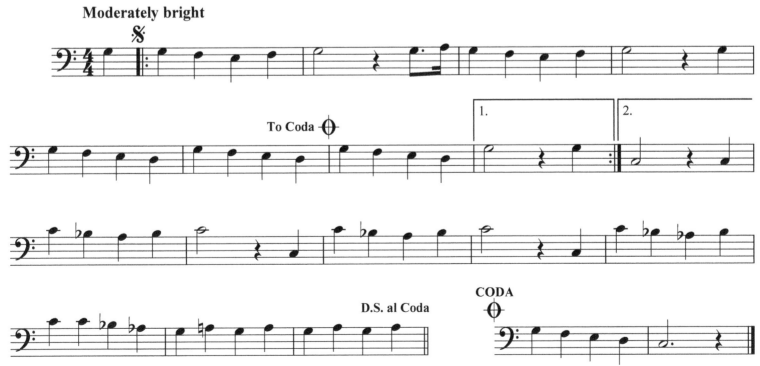

# WHEN SHE LOVED ME

from TOY STORY 2

TROMBONE

Music and Lyrics by
RANDY NEWMAN

**Tenderly, very freely**

# WHEN YOU WISH UPON A STAR
from PINOCCHIO

TROMBONE

Words by NED WASHINGTON
Music by LEIGH HARLINE

**Moderately**

# WHEN WILL MY LIFE BEGIN?

from TANGLED

TROMBONE

Music by ALAN MENKEN
Lyrics by GLENN SLATER

**Moderately, in 2**

**Moderately slow (in 4)**

**Slowly, freely**

# WITH A SMILE AND A SONG
from SNOW WHITE AND THE SEVEN DWARFS

Words by LARRY MOREY
Music by FRANK CHURCHILL

**Moderately slow, in 2**

# WHO'S AFRAID OF THE BIG BAD WOLF?

from THREE LITTLE PIGS

TROMBONE

Words and Music by
FRANK CHURCHILL
Additional Lyric by ANN RONELL

**Moderately, in 2**

# WINNIE THE POOH
from THE MANY ADVENTURES OF WINNIE THE POOH

**TROMBONE**

Words and Music by RICHARD M. SHERMAN
and ROBERT B. SHERMAN

**Tenderly**

# A WHOLE NEW WORLD

from ALADDIN

**TROMBONE**

Music by ALAN MENKEN
Lyrics by TIM RICE

# THE WONDERFUL THING ABOUT TIGGERS

TROMBONE

from THE MANY ADVENTURES OF WINNIE THE POOH

Words and Music by RICHARD M. SHERMAN
and ROBERT B. SHERMAN

**Very brightly**

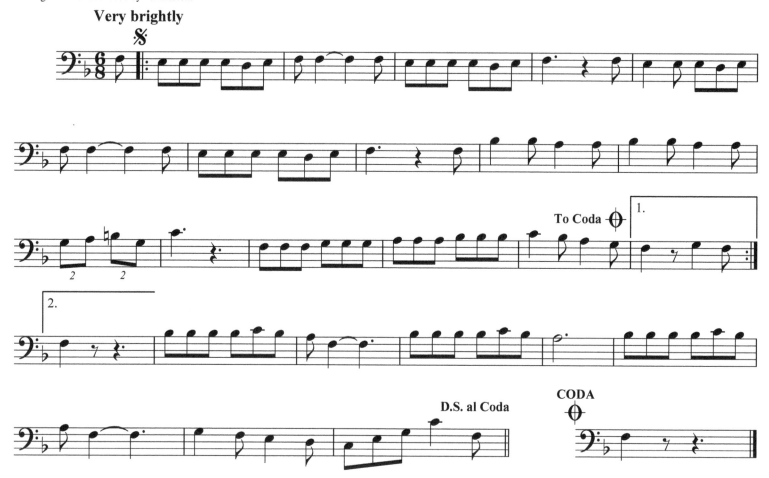

# YO HO

## (A Pirate's Life for Me)

from Disney Parks' Pirates of the Caribbean attraction

Words by XAVIER ATENCIO
Music by GEORGE BRUNS

**In a robust manner**

# THEME FROM ZORRO
from the Television Series

Words by NORMAN FOSTER
Music by GEORGE BRUNS

**Moderately, in 2**

# WRITTEN IN THE STARS
from AIDA

TROMBONE

Music by ELTON JOHN
Lyrics by TIM RICE

# YOU CAN FLY! YOU CAN FLY! YOU CAN FLY!

TROMBONE

from PETER PAN

Words by SAMMY CAHN
Music by SAMMY FAIN

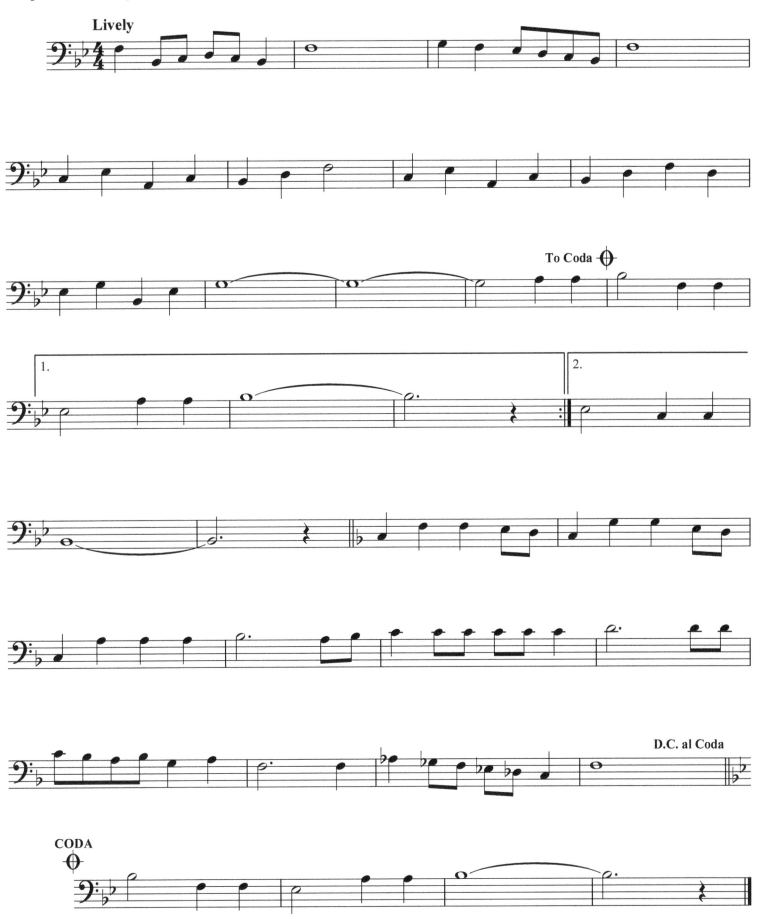

# YOU ARE THE MUSIC IN ME

from HIGH SCHOOL MUSICAL 2

TROMBONE

Words and Music by
JAMIE HOUSTON

**Moderately fast Rock**

# YOU'LL BE IN MY HEART
(Pop Version)
from TARZAN™

TROMBONE

Words and Music by
PHIL COLLINS

**Moderately**

CODA

# YOU'RE WELCOME
## from MOANA

**TROMBONE**

Music and Lyrics by
LIN-MANUEL MIRANDA

# ZIP-A-DEE-DOO-DAH
from SONG OF THE SOUTH

Words by RAY GILBERT
Music by ALLIE WRUBEL

**Brightly**

# ZERO TO HERO
from HERCULES

TROMBONE

Music by ALAN MENKEN
Lyrics by DAVID ZIPPEL

**Driving 4**

# YOU'VE GOT A FRIEND IN ME

from TOY STORY

TROMBONE

Music and Lyrics by
RANDY NEWMAN